READING POWER

Record-Breaking Animals

The Blue Whale
World's Largest Mammal

Joy Paige

The Rosen Publishing Group's
PowerKids Press™
New York

Published in 2002 by The Rosen Publishing Group, Inc.
29 East 21st Street, New York, NY 10010

First Edition

Book Design: Sam Jordan

Photo Credits: Cover, pp. 7, 12–13, 18–19 © Mike Johnson; pp. 5, 8–9 © Innerspace Visions; p. 9 © Kim Sayer/Corbis; pp. 10–11 © Corbis; pp. 14–15, 17 © Animals Animals; pp. 20–21 © Noaa.gov

Paige, Joy.
The blue whale : world's largest mammal / by Joy Paige.
    p. cm. – (Record-Breaking Animals)
Includes bibliographical references and index.
ISBN 0-8239-5962-7 (lib. bdg.)
1. Blue whale–Juvenile literature. [1. Blue whale. 2. Whales.] I. Title.
QL737.C424 P32 2002
599.5'248–dc21
                                                    2001000168

Manufactured in the United States of America

Contents

The Largest Mammal

The blue whale is the largest mammal.

Blue whales live in oceans all over the world. They are on the endangered species list.

Arctic
Ocean

North
Atlantic
Ocean

North
Pacific
Ocean

North
Pacific
Ocean

Indian
Ocean

South
Pacific
Ocean

South
Atlantic
Ocean

Blue whales can grow to be over 100 feet long. Their hearts are the size of small cars.

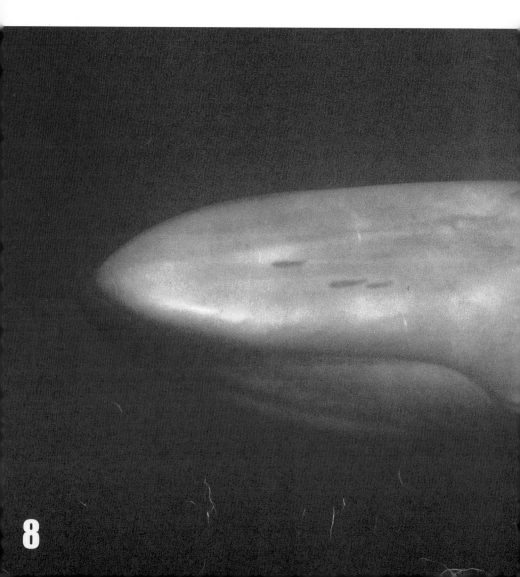

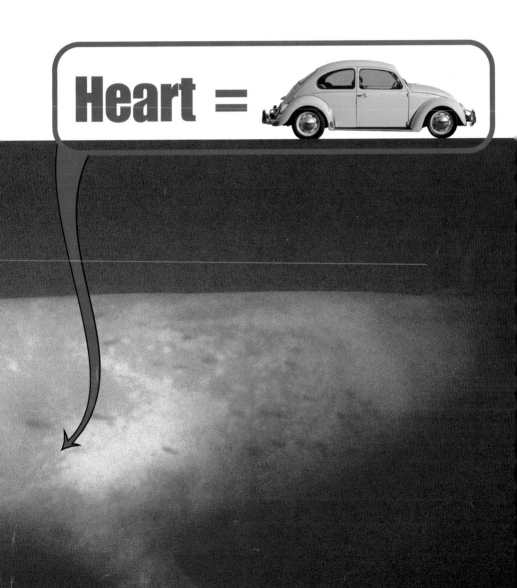

Heart =

Blue whales are heavy. They can weigh between 200,000 and 300,000 pounds. That is the weight of 21 elephants!

Blue whale babies are called calves. Calves are about 23 feet long and weigh about 5,000 pounds when they are born.

13

Swimming

Blue whales have very large tails. Their tails help them swim fast. Blue whales can swim up to 30 miles an hour.

Blue whales breathe from two blowholes on the top of their bodies. Blue whales can hold their breath for an hour!

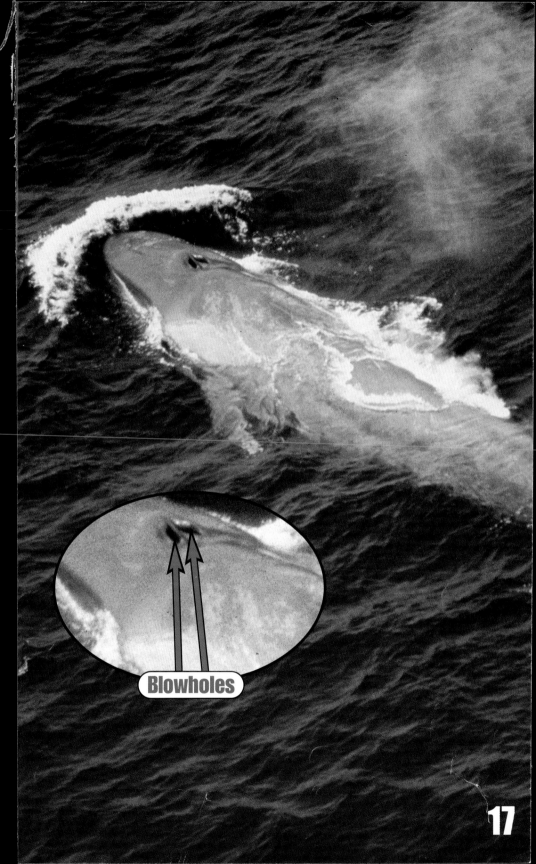

Blowholes

Food

Blue whales eat other sea animals. Their favorite food is krill. Sometimes they eat as much as 40 million krill a day!

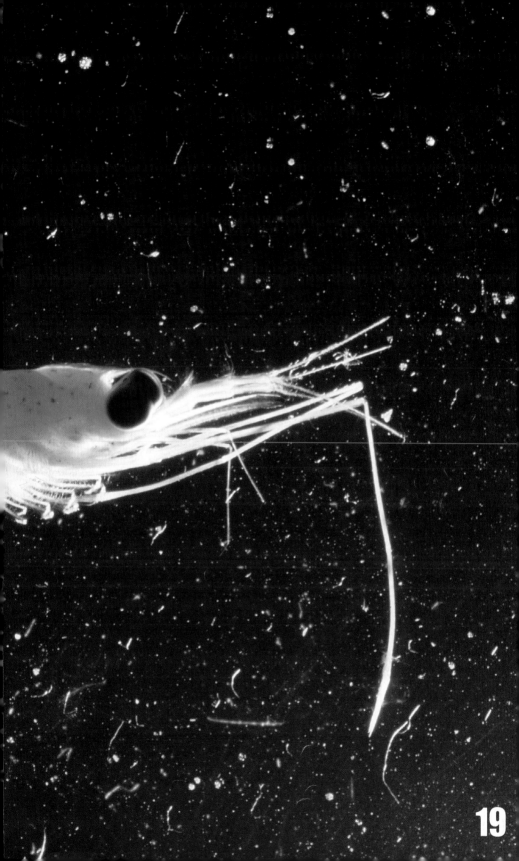

The blue whale is the largest
mammal that has ever lived!

21

Glossary

blowholes (**bloh**-hohlz) the openings on a whale's head that allow air in

breathe (**breeth**) to take air into the lungs and force it out

calves (**cavz**) baby whales

endangered species (en-**dane**-jurhd **spee**-ceez) a group of animals or plants that might stop living on Earth

krill (**krihl**) a type of sea life that whales eat

mammal (**mam**-uhl) a warm-blooded animal

Resources

Books

Blue Whales
by Patricia Miller-Schroeder
Raintree Steck-Vaughn Publishers (1998)

The Blue Whale
by Melissa Kim
Hambleton-Hill Publishing (1993)

Web Site

All About Whales!
http://www.enchantedlearning.com/
   subjects/whales/

Index

B
blowholes, 16–17

C
calves, 12

H
heart, 8–9

K
krill, 18

M
mammal, 4, 20

O
ocean, 6–7

T
tails, 14

Word Count: 157

Note to Librarians, Teachers, and Parents

If reading is a challenge, Reading Power is a solution! Reading Power is perfect for readers who want high-interest subject matter at an accessible reading level. These fact-filled, photo-illustrated books are designed for readers who want straightforward vocabulary, engaging topics, and a manageable reading experience. With clear picture/text correspondence, leveled Reading Power books put the reader in charge. Now readers have the power to get the information they want and the skills they need in a user-friendly format.